WELCOME TO AUSTRALIA

COUNTRIES OF THE WORLD

Australia

by Rebecca Sabelko

BLASTOFF! READERS 2

BELLWETHER MEDIA • MINNEAPOLIS, MN

Blastoff! Readers are carefully developed by literacy experts to build reading stamina and move students toward fluency by combining standards-based content with developmentally appropriate text.

LEVELS

Level 1 provides the most support through repetition of high-frequency words, light text, predictable sentence patterns, and strong visual support.

Level 2 offers early readers a bit more challenge through varied sentences, increased text load, and text-supportive special features.

Level 3 advances early-fluent readers toward fluency through increased text load, less reliance on photos, advancing concepts, longer sentences, and more complex special features.

★ **Blastoff! Universe**

Reading Level: Grade K → Grades 1–3 → Grade 4

This edition first published in 2023 by Bellwether Media, Inc.

No part of this publication may be reproduced in whole or in part without written permission of the publisher. For information regarding permission, write to Bellwether Media, Inc., Attention: Permissions Department, 6012 Blue Circle Drive, Minnetonka, MN 55343.

Library of Congress Cataloging-in-Publication Data

Names: Sabelko, Rebecca, author.
Title: Australia / by Rebecca Sabelko.
Description: Minneapolis, MN : Bellwether Media, Inc., 2023. | Series: Blastoff! Readers : countries of the world | Includes bibliographical references and index. | Audience: Ages 5-8 | Audience: Grades 2-3 | Summary: "Relevant images match informative text in this introduction to Australia. Intended for students in kindergarten through third grade"– Provided by publisher.
Identifiers: LCCN 2022018170 (print) | LCCN 2022018171 (ebook) | ISBN 9781644877135 (library binding) | ISBN 9781648347597 (ebook)
Subjects: LCSH: Australia–Juvenile literature.
Classification: LCC DU96 .S22 2023 (print) | LCC DU96 (ebook) | DDC 994–dc23/eng/20220429
LC record available at https://lccn.loc.gov/2022018170
LC ebook record available at https://lccn.loc.gov/2022018171

Text copyright © 2023 by Bellwether Media, Inc. BLASTOFF! READERS and associated logos are trademarks and/or registered trademarks of Bellwether Media, Inc.

Editor: Elizabeth Neuenfeldt   Designer: Gabriel Hilger
Printed in the United States of America, North Mankato, MN.

Table of Contents

All About Australia	4
Land and Animals	6
Life in Australia	12
Australia Facts	20
Glossary	22
To Learn More	23
Index	24

All About Australia

Canberra

Australia is a huge country. It is also a **continent**!

The country is between the Indian and Pacific Oceans. Its capital is Canberra.

Land and Animals

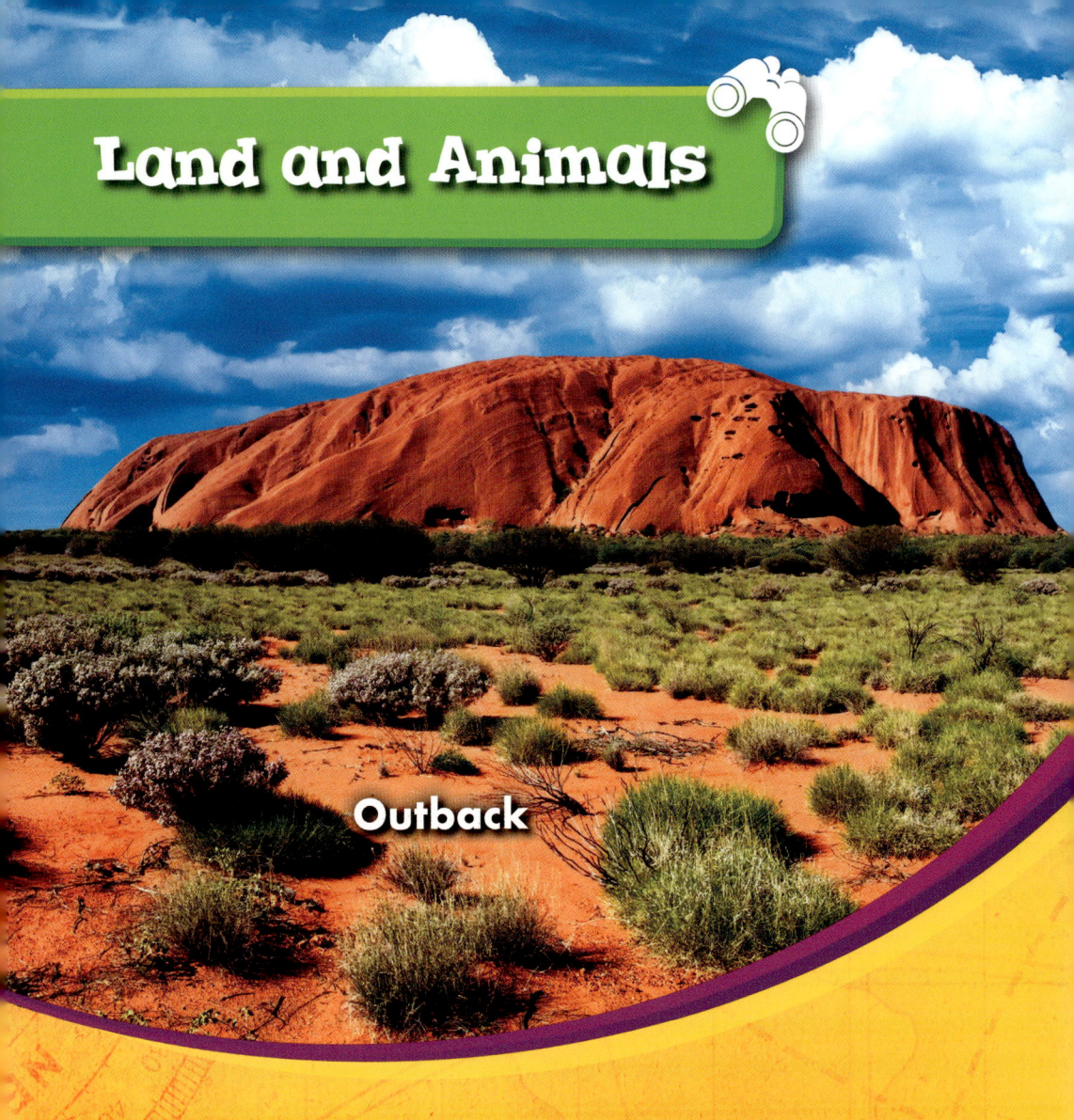

Outback

The **Outback** makes up much of western Australia. It is mostly **deserts**.

Summers can get very hot. Some days may reach over 100 degrees Fahrenheit (38 degrees Celsius)!

The Great Dividing **Range** rises in the east. Snow falls on these low mountains each winter.

The Great Barrier **Reef** lies along the northeastern coast.

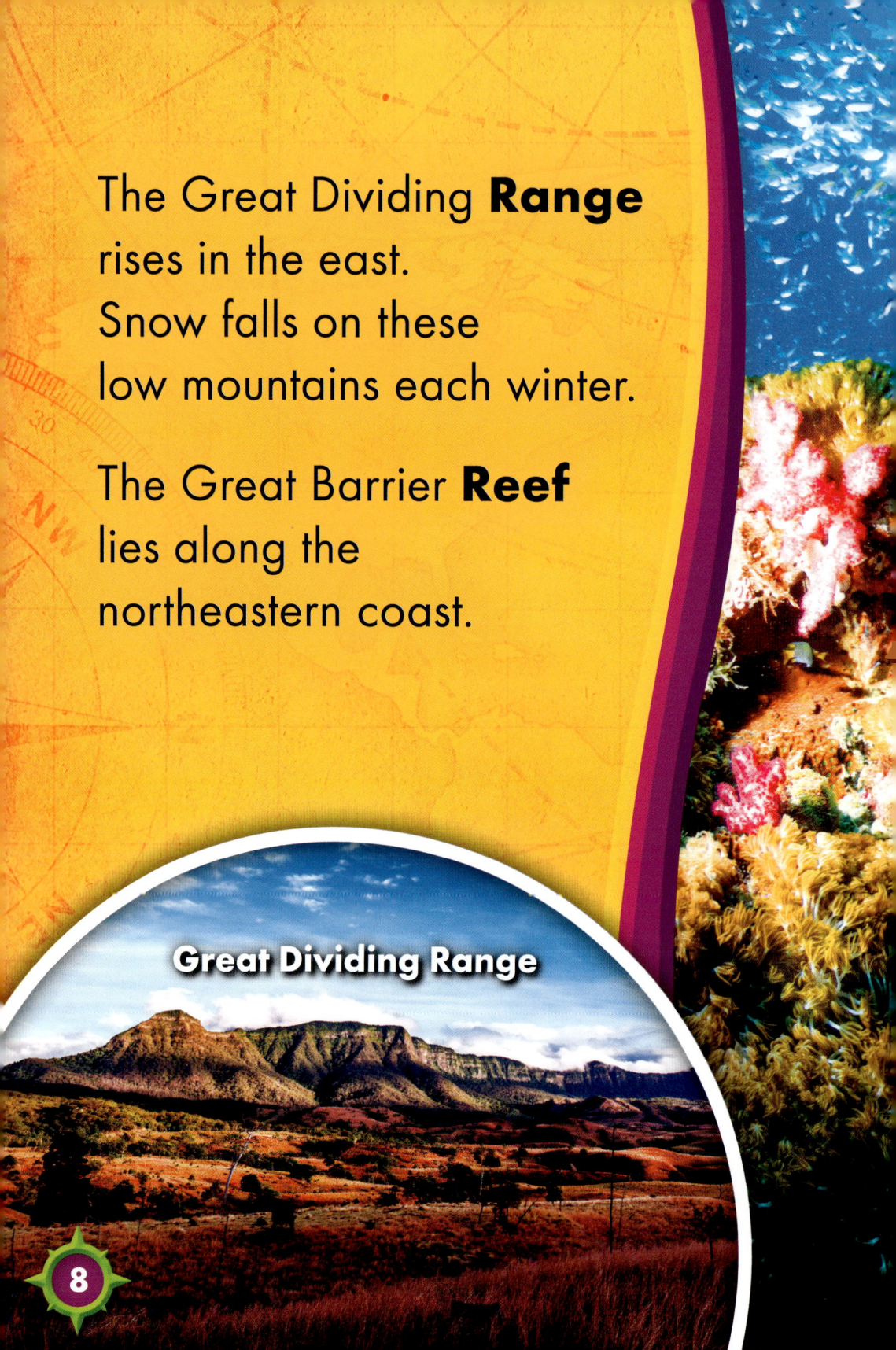

Great Dividing Range

Great Barrier Reef

Size: around 135,000 square miles (350,000 square kilometers)

Famous For: world's largest coral reef

Many animals live in the country. Kookaburras rest in trees. Kangaroos jump across the Outback.

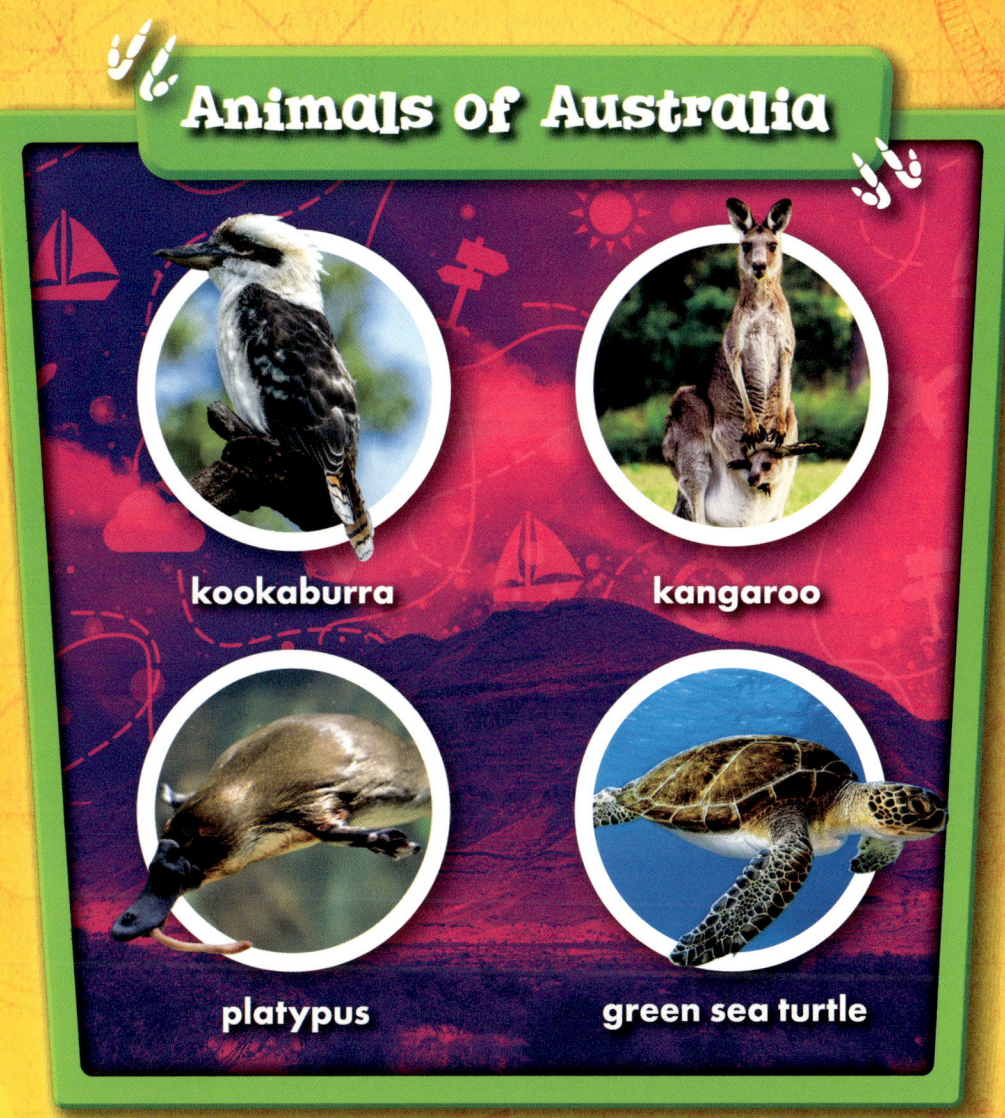

Animals of Australia

kookaburra

kangaroo

platypus

green sea turtle

Platypuses dive to muddy river bottoms. Sea turtles swim through the reef.

Life in Australia

Many Australians have European or Asian backgrounds. **Aboriginal and Torres Strait Islander** peoples call the country home.

Most of the country's **population** lives in cities. Australians mostly speak English.

Melbourne

cricket

People like cricket and rugby. *Boogalah* is a game that began in the country.

People surf along the coasts. They enjoy a **barbie** with friends.

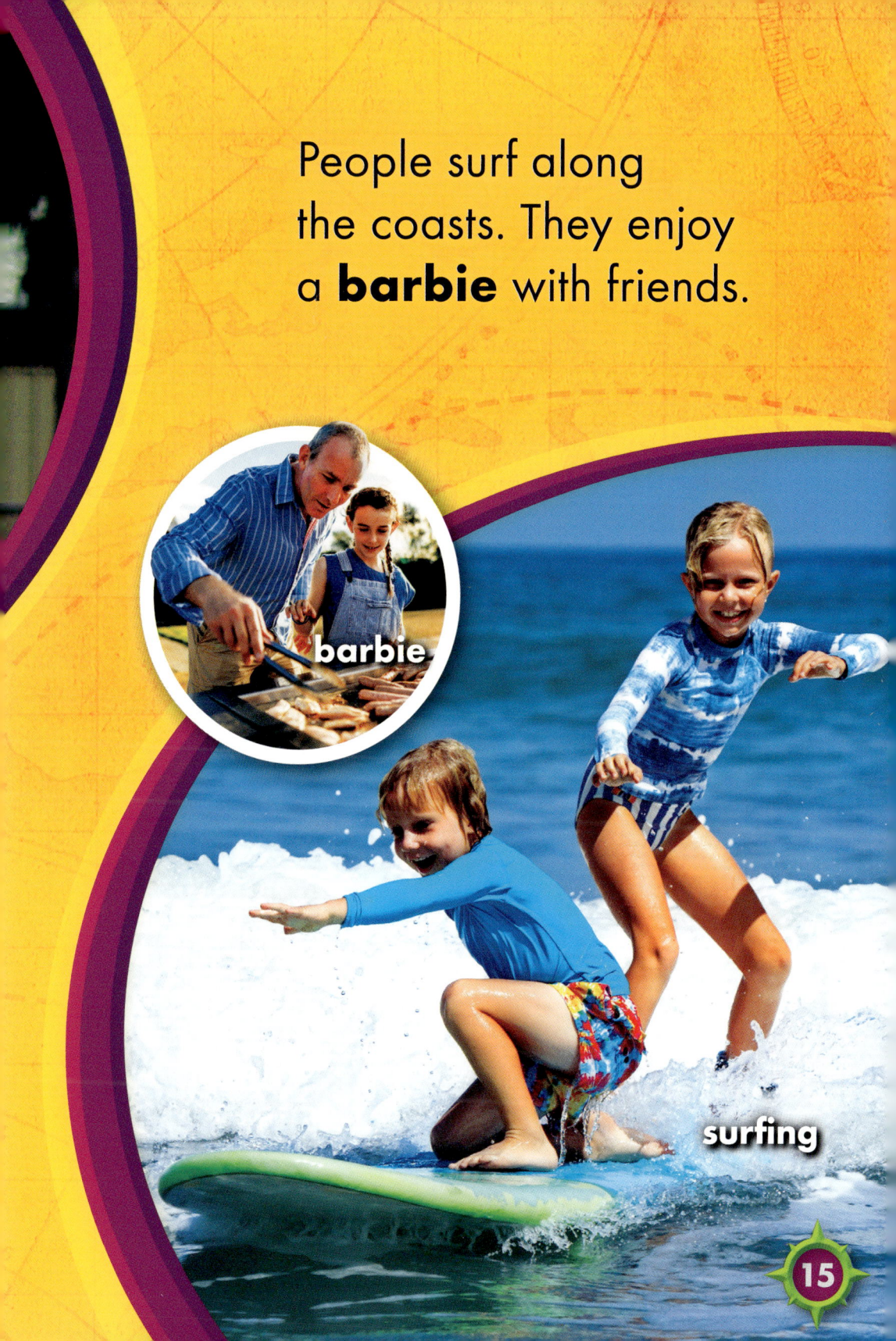

People put Vegemite on toast. Meat pies are a favorite snack.

Australian Foods

Vegemite on toast

meat pies

witchetty grubs

lamingtons

witchetty grubs

Witchetty grubs are an **ancient** food. They taste like nuts! Lamingtons are sweet cakes.

Australia Day is January 26.
It is Australia's national holiday.
People race sailboats!

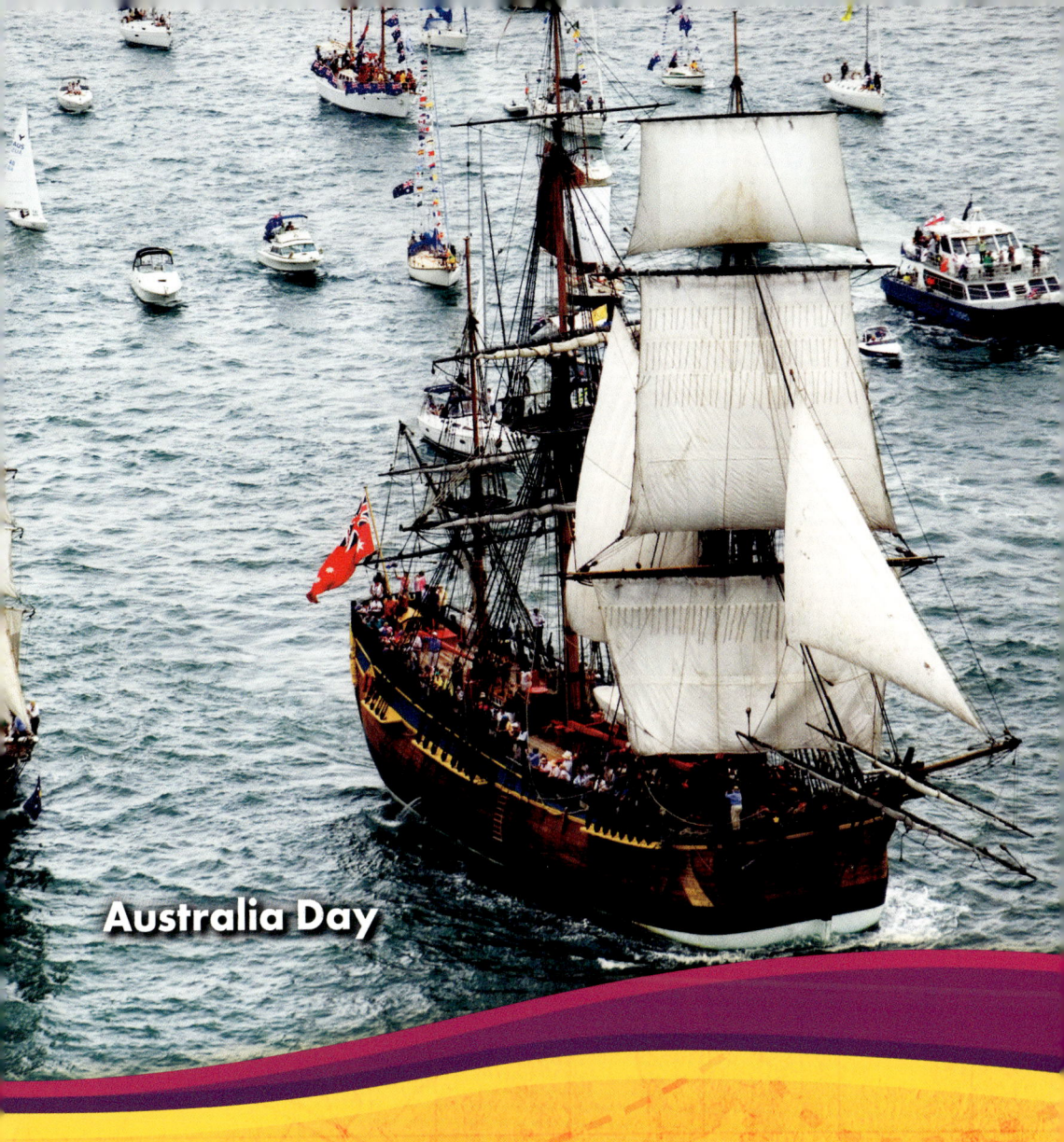

Australia Day

Anzac Day is April 25. People honor the **armed forces**. Holidays bring Australians together!

Australia Facts

Size:
2,988,902 square miles
(7,741,220 square kilometers)

Population:
26,141,369 (2022)

National Holiday:
Australia Day (January 26)

Main Language:
Australian English

Capital City:
Canberra

Famous Face

Name: Chris Hemsworth

Famous For: an actor in Marvel superhero movies

Religions

- none: 30%
- Protestant: 23%
- other: 24%
- Roman Catholic: 23%

Top Landmarks

Blue Mountains National Park

Sydney Opera House

Uluru

Glossary

Aboriginal and Torres Strait Islander—related to the different groups of people who have lived in Australia from the earliest time

ancient—from long ago

armed forces—the military of a country

barbie—a gathering where food is cooked over an open fire

continent—a very large area of land; there are seven continents in the world.

deserts—dry lands with few plants and little rainfall

Outback—the large area in western Australia where few people live

population—the total number of people who live in a certain place

range—a group of mountains

reef—a grouping of rocks or coral in shallow water

To Learn More

AT THE LIBRARY
Duling, Kaitlyn. *Kangaroos*. Minneapolis, Minn.: Bellwether Media, 2021.

Reynolds, Alison. *Your Passport to Australia*. North Mankato, Minn.: Capstone, 2022.

Wilkins, Veronica B. *Explore Australia*. Minneapolis, Minn.: Jump!, 2020.

ON THE WEB

Factsurfer.com gives you a safe, fun way to find more information.

1. Go to www.factsurfer.com.
2. Enter "Australia" into the search box and click 🔍.
3. Select your book cover to see a list of related content.

Index

Aboriginal and Torres Strait Islander, 12
animals, 10, 11
Anzac Day, 19
Australia Day, 18, 19
Australia facts, 20–21
barbie, 15
boogalah, 14
Canberra, 4, 5
capital (see Canberra)
cities, 12
coast, 8, 15
continent, 4
cricket, 14
deserts, 6
English, 12, 13
foods, 16, 17
Great Barrier Reef, 8, 9, 11

Great Dividing Range, 8
Indian Ocean, 5
map, 5
Outback, 6, 10
Pacific Ocean, 5
people, 12, 14, 15, 16, 18, 19
rugby, 14
say hello, 13
summers, 7
surf, 15
winter, 8

The images in this book are reproduced through the courtesy of: Tooykrub, front cover; Dianne Wickenden, front cover; Rob Wilson, p. 3; zetter, pp. 4-5; Claudio Soldi, pp. 6-7; Adwo, p. 7; Janelle Lugge, p. 8; Colin Baker/ Getty Images, pp. 8-9; Freder, pp. 10-11; Nick Brundle Photography, p. 11 (kookaburra); IntoTheWorld, p. 11 (kangaroo); JohnCarnemolla, p. 11 (platypus), 22-23; Ed Jenkins, p. 11 (green sea turtle); Gordon Bell, p. 12; noBorders - Brayden Howie, pp. 12-13; Russotwins/ Alamy, pp. 14-15; SolStock, p. 15 (inset); Denis Moskvinov, p. 15; gowithstock, p. 16 (Vegemite); kucherAV, p. 16 (meat pies); bennymarty, p. 16 (witchetty grubs); BBA Photography, p. 16 (lamingtons); Hilke Maunder/ Alamy, p. 17; Travelscape Images/ Alamy, pp. 18-19; titoOnz, p. 20 (flag); Tinseltown, p. 20 (Chris Hemsworth); ian woolcock, p. 21 (Blue Mountains National Park); travellight, p. 21 (Sydney Opera House); bmphotographer, p. 21 (Uluru).